The Mysteries

By Annie Besant

Copyright © 2021 Lamp of Trismegistus. All rights reserved. No part of this publication may be reproduced or transmitted in any form or by any means, electronic or mechanical, including photocopying, recording, or by any information storage and retrieval system, without permission in writing from Lamp of Trismegistus. Reviewers may quote brief passages.

ISBN: 978-1-63118-572-4

Esoteric Classics

Other Books in this Series and Related Titles

Aurora of the Philosophers by Paracelsus (978-1-63118-507-6)

Clairvoyance and Psychic Abilities by A Besant &c (978-1-63118-403-1)

The Feminine Occult by various authors (978-1-63118-711-7)

Rosicrucian Rules, Secret Signs, Codes and Symbols by various (978-1-63118-488-8)

An Outline of Theosophy by C W Leadbeater (978-1-63118-452-9)

Paracelsus, the Four Elements and Their Spirits by M P Hall (978-1-63118-400-0)

Essays on Ancient Magic by Helena P Blavatsky (978-1-63118-535-9)

Essays on the Esoteric Tradition of Karma by A Besant &c (978-1-63118-426-0)

The Use of Evil by Annie Besant (978-1-63118-532-8)

The Alchemical Catechism of Paracelsus by Paracelsus (978-1-63118-513-7)

Alchemy in the Nineteenth Century by Helena P Blavatsky (978-1-63118-446-8)

Qabbalistic Teachings and the Tree of Life by M P Hall (978-1-63118-482-6)

The Historic, Mythic and Mystic Christ by Annie Besant (978–1–63118–533–5)

The Hidden Mysteries of Christianity by Annie Besant (978–1–63118–534–2)

History, Analysis and Secret Tradition of the Tarot by Hall &c (978-1-63118-445-1)

Crystal Vision Through Crystal Gazing by Frater Achad (978-1-63118-455-0)

The Golden Verses of Pythagoras: Five Translations (978-1-63118-479-6)

Arcane Formulas or Mental Alchemy by W W Atkinson (978-1-63118-459-8)

The Machinery of the Mind by Dion Fortune (978-1-63118-451-2)

The A E Waite Reader: A Selection of Occult Essays (978-1-63118-515-1)

The Leadbeater Reader: A Selection of Occult Essays (978-1-63118-483-3)

Audio versions are also available on Audible, Amazon and Apple

Other Books in this Series and Related Titles

Fundamental Ideas of Theosophy by Bhagwan Das (978–1–63118–571–7)

Dreams: What They Are and How They Are Caused (978–1–63118–570–0)

Communication Between Different Worlds by Annie Besant (978–1–63118–569–4)

Animism, Magic and the Omnipotence of Thought by S Freud (978–1–63118–568–7)

Buddhism by F Otto Schrader (978–1–63118–567–0)

Death by W W Westcott (978–1–63118–566–3)

The Religion of Theosophy by Bhagwan Das (978–1–63118–565–6)

The Spirit of Zoroastrianism by Henry S Olcott (978–1–63118–564–9)

The Brotherhood of Religions by Annie Besant (978–1–63118–563–2)

Fourth Book of Maccabees by Josephus (978-1-63118-562-5)

The Story of Ahikar by Ahiqar (978-1-63118-561-8)

Vision of the Spirit by C. Jinarajadasa (978-1-63118-560-1)

Occult Arts by William Q. Judge (978-1-63118-559-5)

Kali the Mother by Sister Nivedita (978-1-63118-558-8)

Love and Death by Sri Aurobindo (978–1–63118–557–1)

Times and Seasons Volume 1, Numbers 4-6 (978-1-63118-556-4)

The Book of John Whitmer by John Whitmer (978-1-63118-554-0)

Interesting Account of Several Remarkable Visions (978-1-63118-553-3)

The Evening and Morning Star Volume 1, Numbers 11 & 12 (978-1-63118-552-6)

Private Diary of Joseph Smith 1832-1834 (978-1-63118-546-5)

A Manuscript on Far West by Reed Peck (978-1-63118-544-1)

Audio versions are also available on Audible, Amazon and Apple

Table of Contents

Introduction...7

The Mysteries...9

The Value of Devotion...29

INTRODUCTION

The word "esoteric" can be difficult to define. Esotericism in general can be seen less as a system of beliefs and more as a category, which encompasses numerous, different systems of beliefs. It's a bit of juxtaposition, since the word "esoteric" indicates something that few people know about, while the term itself broadly covers numerous philosophies, practices, areas of study and belief systems.

In a greater sense, Esotericism acts as a storehouse for secret knowledge, which is often considered ancient (by *tradition, if not by fact),* passed down from generation to generation, in private. At various times in history, simply possessing the knowledge of some of these subjects, was considered illegal and a jailable offence, if discovered. This usually included such general topics as Alchemy, Pharmacology, Qabalah, Hermeticism, Occultism, Ceremonial Magic, Astrology, Divination, Rosicrucianism and so on. Collectively, these areas of study were often referred to as the esoteric sciences.

Sometimes, the outer garment of a subject isn't esoteric, while what is hidden beneath it, is. As an example, Freemasonry isn't necessarily esoteric by nature (at *least not anymore),* but certain signs, passwords and handshakes given to the candidate during their initiation, are in fact, esoteric, in the sense that they are hidden from the general public.

Today, in the twenty-first century, such topics are readily available at bookstores across the country, and numerous mainsteam publishers offer beginners guides and coffee-table volumes on many of these subjects, intended for mass appeal. Books like *"The Secret"* have turned previously arcane topics into household knowledge. All that being the case, however, it isn't to say that there still aren't buried secrets to uncover, ancient wisdom being ignored and forgotten mysteries to be explored. In fact, it is often that we are only able to further our own studies by standing on the shoulders of these disappearing giants.

Lamp of Trismegistus is doing its part to help preserve humanity's esoteric history by making some of these classics available to those students who are seeking to unearth the knowledge of these ancient colossi.

So, be sure to check other titles from our *Esoteric Classics* series, as well as our *Occult Fiction, Theosophical Classics, Foundations of Freemasonry Series, Supernatural Fiction, Paranormal Research Series, Studies in Buddhism* and our *Christian Apocrypha Series*. You can also download the audio versions of most of these titles from Amazon, Apple or Audible, for learning on the go.

THE MYSTERIES

Many and diverse have been and are the religions of the past and the present, the religions living and dead. One great difference one perceives in looking back over the history of the older past and comparing it with the history of more modern days: in the ancient times one does not come across anything in history of the nature of persecution of faith by faith. You find that each religion has its own kingdom, its own area, over which it rules. You find that a nation has its own faith, and that that faith lives in amity with other faiths of neighboring nations, unless it chanced that the nations themselves were at war. You find in imperial Rome, for instance, that a great Pantheon was raised, in which the Gods of every nation within the Roman Empire found each his place and each his cult. There might sometimes be jealousies and envies, but there was no idea that one religion was to rule over every nation; but rather that each nation naturally had its own particular faith and that the people of the nation worshipped their national God.

You find, looking back to those days, that if there was any trouble with regard to religion, then the origin of the trouble was political rather than religious. To leave the religion of the nation was equivalent to treason to the State; and so now and again you may find a man attacked and banished because of a change of faith. But that was rather because he denied his fatherland than because there was any wrong in thinking along his own lines on a question of belief; and it, is very noticeable that, in some of the most ancient faiths, it was held that, so far as intellectual acceptance of doctrine was concerned, the intellect might have free play, and there was no limit to the area over which the thought might extend.

On the other hand, in comparatively modern days, you find that religious persecution plays a great part in the history of rival faiths. You find many a missionary effort, many attempts to convert other peoples to a religion which is not the religion of their ancestors, and one not unnaturally demands: "Why this difference in the matter of tolerance between the ancient world and the comparatively modern? Why has this idea arisen that all people should accept a particular presentment of truth, that they should not follow an ancestral faith, but rather embrace one which is brought to them from other lands?"

And it is not without significance that the tendency to persecute in relation to religion is historically contemporaneous with the disappearance of the Mysteries from Europe. It was in connection with their gradual disappearance that you find arising the specter of religious persecution, so that one is inclined to put the two phenomena side by side, and to ask whether there may not be a relation between the disappearance of the Mysteries and the appearance of persecution.

When we come to enquire as to the difference between the exoteric faith and the esoteric teaching, when we come to look into the faiths of the past and to study the Mysteries of the past, we find that the faiths were just as different in the older world as they are different in the modern; but we also find that in relation to every faith there were Mysteries established, to which the most learned of that faith belonged, and in which the teachers of that faith were trained. We find, as we study still further, that though the outer presentment of religious doctrines in the exoteric faith differed with the nation, with the temperament and the traditions of the people, the teaching which made the Knower, the teaching which educated the Mystic, the teaching which gave knowledge instead of belief and enabled a man with full certainty to declare: "I know the things of the super-physical worlds" — we find that that teaching was everywhere one and the same, and that while the various exoteric faiths might differ, the inner heart of them, as found in the Mysteries, was the same. Just as you might, if you wandered round some great cathedral, see the light pouring out from window after window, and through every window a different color; as you might say, looking at that light streaming out through the glass: "The light in the temple is red", and another might cry: "The light in the temple is blue", and another would declare: "Nay, but the light is yellow", while another would asseverate that the light was purple; so with the exoteric religions of the world, each has its own color, each has its own presentment, and those who only see the outer religion declare that the religions differ, and that the light of truth that comes through each is not one and the same.

But just as if you go within the cathedral, if you penetrate within the shrine, you see that one white light is there and that the difference of the color is in the windows and not in the light, so do you see, when you enter into the Temple of the Mysteries, that truth is one though it may be presented in different fashions, and that though the colors of the faiths are various as the hues of the rainbow, inside the Temple of the Mysteries the white Light of Truth is one and the same. And it is, I think, because of that knowledge — which, inasmuch as it is knowledge of facts, cannot vary, while the language in which the facts are told will vary according to the speaker — it is because in all the ancient religions there was ever at the heart of them the Mysteries, giving the unity of truth and the unity of knowledge, it was because of that, that persecution for religious belief did not stain the older world; for the teachers knew there was the one truth, although the peoples might differ in their understanding of that truth veiled in garments of dogma, of ceremony, of varied presentment.

So one begins to think, if we are again in modern days to persuade the living religions of the world that they should form a Brotherhood and not a battlefield of warring creeds, that we must find a common place where all the religions may find their origin, where all the religions may find their teachers. We must hope and labor and aspire that that ancient institution of the Mysteries may once more be restored for the lighting and the helping of the world, and we must endeavor so to study and so to live that pupils may be found who shall draw down the Teachers from on high by the passion of their aspiration, by the purity of their lives, by the depth of their knowledge, who may thus show themselves worthy to be taught again by Men made perfect, to draw among themselves as Teachers, Those who have knowledge more than the knowledge of men.

Let us think, then, what the Mysteries were in reality. Let us glance for a few moments at the phases through which they have passed, and let us ask whether in our modern days it be possible to find material out of which pupils can be found to be taught. Never in the higher worlds is there grudging in the giving of the truth; never from above comes the check which prevents the pouring out of knowledge over the world. It is here, here in our lower world, here in these minds of men resistant of truth which they find it difficult to grasp; it is in the challenging, constantly questioning mind of our modern days; it is here that lies the difficulty in the restoration of the Mysteries; it is here that the barriers have been built up which check the free flow of truth.

This is not to be regarded as though it were outside the great Plan of the King of Evolution. There is naught outside that Plan; and if sometimes we think that things go ill, it is because our eyes are short-sighted, because we are not able to see the whole, and we judge only by a portion that we see. For in the great evolution of mankind, which lasts through millennium after millennium of our mortal time, in which days are tens of thousands of years, and in which a million years are but as yesterday to those great Minds that see over the whole of evolution; in the working out of such a Plan, in a gradual development of one stage after another, there is no stage which may be missed, there is no stage that is evil; each has its place in the long evolution, and the Architect who drew the Plan knows well the building that He is intending to erect.

It was necessary for human growth, necessary for the higher evolution of men, that there should be a period during which this mind of ours should develop the questioning, challenging, rebellious spirit without which it would not have conquered the knowledge of this lower world. It was well enough in days long gone by that child-nations should look up to divine Instructors, and obediently study the lessons given to them by those divine Men. But it was also well that the growing youth should develop the powers of manhood; and he could not have done it, had he always been kept in the leading-strings of Those greater than himself. So the time came when the Teachers said to the boy: "Go out, my son, into the world and find out for yourself what is the truth; develop within yourself the mind which is one aspect of the divine Spirit, and conquer by your own unaided strength the knowledge which the world can unveil before you; yours it is to conquer the lower world, yours it is to discover the laws of nature, yours it is to find your way while the guide for the moment is hidden."

But just as the father who sends out his son into the world watches over him with tender love and is ever ready to help when advice is needed, so was it with the Fathers of the race, those Elder Brethren who had reached perfection before the younger had climbed the ladder of evolution. They have ever been watching, although out of sight, withdrawn from physical vision but ever near and ready to help, and They have guided the nations as much through the times when Their forms were hidden, as They guided them when dwelling in the City of the Golden Gates of Atlantis, or in the White City of Shambala at the origins of our Aryan Race.

But the times are changed and with the changing times a changing method. It has been said, and rightly said, that evolution is not a ladder of ascent but rather a spiral that ever returns upon itself higher and higher as evolution climbs. So it is that the past becomes again the present, but the present on a higher level than the road that humanity in the past has trodden, and the times are approaching when the Mysteries shall again be restored to earth, for the pupils are preparing today, and when the pupil is ready, as the old saying runs, the Master appears.

Think, then, of the times when the Mysteries were established on our globe and realize what was their function and their work. The outer religion, the religion of law of command, the religion that said "Thou shalt", or "Thou shalt not", that is, the outer religion that guides a man to righteous conduct by an authority imposed upon him from without, by moral codes, by laws of conduct which the man obeys oft- times without understanding their reason, obeys because a great Prophet has said so, because a Scripture has been written giving the precept, because a Church has proclaimed commandments, because a Tradition has declared: "This is the way, walk ye in it" — such a line of instruction, such a moral code, such a system of laws, makes the good man; makes the man who is the worthy citizen of the State, the man who is the loving husband and father in the home, the man who is ever ready to work for his country, who is looked up to as one of character and of noble life. But that is not the highest. A wise man in days long gone by declared: "The law was our schoolmaster to bring us unto Christ". A time comes in human evolution, when the work of the outer law is over because the law of the Spirit is unfolding from within, when the man no longer walks by an outer compulsion but by an inner direction, when the God within speaks, instead of the God without; and it is the function of the Mysteries to unfold the God within and to change man into the man made perfect, the man in whom the hidden God shines forth with manifested glory.

So we may read with reference to the Schools of Pythagoras that there were many who learned the outer teachings, who learned the civil and the social virtues, and so became the patterns of virtue that were the glory of ancient Greece. But that was only the outer court of the Temple; that was on the worldly side of the threshold of the Mysteries. For we read that there were other Schools, secret and hidden, into which, those who had reached goodness might be admitted, and in which the good man was developed into the God. That was the object of the Mysteries: to take the good man who had conquered all ordinary temptations, who had grown to a point where the world no longer either deceived or attracted, who had been able to develop within himself those essential virtues which are the bases on which everything else is to be erected — to take that man, to let him step over the threshold into the Temple. There they instructed him how the God within might unfold his powers, and how his garments of matter might be constructed so as to be vehicles for the forces of God instead of hindrances to those forces, as they are in the mass of the people in the world.

And then the man was taught, first of all, that he must purify the garments of matter that he was wearing, not only from the ordinary sins of men, not only from the ordinary passions of human kind, but that he must purify garment after garment of subtler and subtler matter, and learn to distinguish himself from the garments that clothed him, and consciously and deliberately to live in the house of matter of which he was the tenant and not the prisoner. For most men live as prisoners in the house of flesh that they wear.

They know not that there is a key that can open the gates; they know not that the key is hidden within themselves and is not held by anyone without. They think that death is the holder of the key, and that only when death comes, with that key which unlocks the body, can the Spirit arise free and immortal and know himself divine.

But in the Mysteries they were taught that the body was not a prison-house but only a dwelling-place; that the key could open the doors and man could walk forth at his will. So first they were taught by deep and profound meditation to draw the life away from the outer garments, and for a time to fix it in the inner and subtler garments that the Spirit wears. They were taught to separate the coarser from the finer; they were taught to evolve the finer senses as nature has evolved the physical senses for us through endless ages of years; and they were taught that the real powers of sight and of hearing resided in the spiritual man and not in the bodies that he was wearing, that the bodies had to be shaped into organs for the spiritual powers, and that each body was a barrier until the Spirit had redeemed the matter and formed it for its own purposes and as an instrument for itself.

Those true Mysteries which still exist — those which are ruled by the great White Brotherhood, the only people who have the right to say: "Enter", or: "Thou art not yet ready to enter" — those true Mysteries have never been withdrawn from earth, but have ever existed in the hands of these Men made perfect, who introduced Their neophytes into the realities of the higher worlds, and taught them consciously and deliberately to become familiar with those worlds of subtler matter, as the scientist of our days is beginning to become familiar with the physical world in which we live.

And today in those true Mysteries, when the doorway of Initiation is thrown open before the prepared pupil who has been led up to that gateway, the pupil passes out of the physical body, and is initiated first in the astral body, and is tested as to his knowledge of how to deal with the powers of that world, how to use its influences for human service. When you read, as you sometimes do, of the tests of the Mysteries, the ordeals of the Mysteries, realize that those are tests of knowledge and of power, not of the physical endurance which you read of in "occult" stories, the passing through fire, through water, through all the elements here: those are but the first and early tests on the astral plane for the pupil; they are not the tests of the man who has to show that he can control the powers of nature, and that they own him as their ruler because he has gained the knowledge which alone is able to control. For in any world, go where you will, be it this mortal world of men or be it the highest world of Nirvana, there is but one thing that gives power, and that is Knowledge. Knowledge enables men to rule, and, as has been truly said, for the Spirit there is no veil in any kingdom of nature.

Therefore of old was the man who had to pass into the temple of the Mysteries spoken of as the Gnostic, the Knower. And every Initiation means an extension of consciousness, an extension which is gained when one gate lies behind you; and the next gate only opens when the knowledge you have conquered enables you to turn the key in its lock. As you trace on, Initiation after Initiation, you find that in each one the pupil, the aspirant, the Initiate, is admitted to another and higher world, and shows that he is able to wield its powers, to use its influence, and always to seek one object and one alone, that he may become of greater service to his fellowmen and may help those who cannot help themselves to a swifter road of progress, to a shorter way to bliss. For the only justification of gaining knowledge is that you may use it for service; and Those who hold the keys of knowledge will only place them in the hands of anyone when that person has proved himself eager to serve, and has mastered the desires of the lower self imprisoned in the bodies, and surrendered himself to the will of the higher Self that knows no will but God's.

And as we look away from these high Mysteries that are, and that were known in the outer world of the past more than they are today, we find that there were many preparatory Schools, Mysteries of the less real kind, which gradually prepared the pupil for the higher Mysteries, and some of these still exist. There are occult Schools scattered over our world today, and all look up to the one White Brotherhood as that to which they aspire; they pass along many different lines which have been brought down from ancient times, different ways and different methods and different fashions of instruction, but all realize that they are preparing for the real Mysteries, those over which the great Hierarchy presides. And looking back into the past we find that there were many such secondary Mysteries known to exist, although the method of their teaching remains occult or hidden.

We find, for instance, that there was a stage in the evolution of religions, in which the pupils were no longer able at will to leave the outer body and go to the Temple of the Mysteries, where alone the higher Initiation should be given.

Some of you may know that in connection with the Egyptian pyramids there were chambers of Initiation which had no door, for no one might enter there who could not pass through the wall encircling the Temple; such needed no door through which to go, because he came in the subtler body into the presence of the Hierophants of these Mysteries. So in Ireland there are still left some towers which have puzzled antiquarians because there is no way into them; there is no need for a door for the man who has learned to use the subtler bodies, for there is no wall that can exclude him, no door that can be locked against him, nothing that can keep him from going whither he will, nothing which this earth can erect in the way of barriers. So it was the fashion of these Mysteries of old, the grade below the real, just as in the real, that only those who could consciously use the higher bodies could be admitted, that they might pass through to the great Way of Initiation.

But the time came when people could not do that of their own free will, and then another method was used. They were thrown into a mesmeric or hypnotic trance, touched with what was called in Greek antiquity the Thyrsus, a rod at first filled with living fire, the touch of which at once broke the links between the higher and the lower bodies, and set the Spirit free within its subtler vehicle in full consciousness of that higher life.

So you will find sometimes, in ancient fresco or in ancient sculpture, a priest stands holding in his hand a rod and on the top of the rod a cone. It was a form of the Rod of Power which was used, and was passed along the spinal column up to where that enters the head; as the fiery rod passed up the spinal column the subtler body was drawn together and gradually followed the rising rod until, as it touched the head, the body passed out through the skull and then was set free to reach the subtler worlds. And a little later still that power has been lost, as the world is going on its onward way, deeper and deeper into matter. Then only the astral vision is opened and the astral hearing, and living pictures are shown in subtler matter, which image out the realities of the other worlds. No longer the subtler world is traversed, only a picture of that world is shown; but a living picture, giving much of knowledge, and even down to our own days that is a common way of teaching. When the living pictures made by the great Teachers are thus shown, we have past history reproduced; when the great work of building worlds is imaged in the subtler matter of the astral plane, the pupil studies these pictures as they unroll before him, and understands better than words could tell him the reality of that history of the past.

Then, coming still lower down, as even this power was lost by those who were the Hierophants of the Mysteries, there came a stage that you may read of among the Greeks, when that which was to be taught was shown by acting, and not either in the worlds themselves or in the living pictures that imaged them out; when men were taught to act scenes which continued the lessons which had to be learned; when the astral world was shown as a dramatic scene; when the passions were imaged as animals, and when men clothed in animals' skins and wearing animal masks surrounded the candidate for the Mysteries, endeavored to drive him back, and tried to terrify him. And if within him there was the germ of any vice remaining, then that inner traitor in the citadel of the mind answered to the threat without which was made by the actor who was acting the vice, and the man, terrified, seeing the vice figured as it were in an outer form, shrank back and dared not face his enemy, and so failed in his passage through this test which was to try the purity of the candidate.

So these Mysteries went on right into Christian days, and if you will read your early Christian books, read the writings of the Apostolic Fathers, trace them on from those who were the pupils of the Apostles themselves and through succeeding writers, read St. Clement of Alexandria, read the works of Origen so far as we have them, you will find in the early days of Christianity there were the Mysteries, the real Mysteries of Jesus. There were two lines of instruction; there were first the teachings of those who had been instructed, as both Origen and St. Clement write, by word of mouth, in the secret teachings given by the Christ while He lived and worked amongst men. You remember He said to His Apostles: "Unto you it is given to know the Mysteries of the Kingdom of God, but to others in parables". And the modern Church is content with the parables, and does not seem to feel the lack of the inner teachings which explain the Mysteries of God. And those which were received by tradition, handed down from mouth to ear by generation after generation of worthy and saintly men, those formed the first teachings in the Mysteries, the teachings, as Origen said, given in secret by Christ to His own disciples.

Then there were higher Mysteries, where not human but superhuman lips taught the secrets of the higher worlds, and you find St. Ignatius of Antioch — I think it is, or perhaps Irenaeus — declaring that the Angels were the teachers in those early Christian Mysteries, superhuman beings who came to those who had been instructed in the knowledge handed down from mouth to ear, and who were worthy to receive that higher teaching, and to come into direct touch with those denizens of higher worlds. So was it also in

Greece and in Egypt, where those whom Christians call Angels, but whom the older religions spoke of as the Shining Ones, were the teachers and revealed the Mysteries of the higher worlds.

Christianity, as much as any other ancient faith, had Mysteries at the back of the outer religion. Men were baptized into the Christian Church, they passed onwards to the Communion, thus utilizing the outer forms which the Christ had left for the helping of believers. But you may remember how St. Paul declared: "We speak wisdom among those who are perfect", declaring that he did not give the higher teaching to those whom he said, although baptized and communicating Christians, were only babes in Christ. All this passed away; and yet not wholly, for ever the true Mysteries remained; but this difference there was, at least in the western world: there was no open road to the Mysteries, there were no intermediate Schools in which men and women might be instructed — only traditions that such things were or had been; and only here and there was a man, who, having been taught personally and individually, grew strong enough to find his own way to those ever-existing Mysteries of the true Brotherhood of the Masters of the Wisdom. But here and there we still find groups of study. You may trace them through old and Middle Age literature, and one word I may give you as a key, for you will often come across it and perhaps not understand quite what it means When you find among some old books a book which is called a Rosary, you have the name by which the secret books were marked out right through the Middle Ages, in which the alchemist and the astrologer and the searcher after secret wisdom wrote down in glyph and symbol the truths that he knew but dare not openly teach. For we are coming to the days of persecution, when men dared not say the things they knew for fear the exoteric faith should crush them, and the carnal knowledge should destroy the spiritual truth. But still here and there a group is to be found, for never was the succession quite destroyed even upon the earth; but men did not know where to look, they searched far and wide and found not a teacher. For they who knew dreaded to communicate their knowledge, lest the pupil should only be a spy or a traitor, and should betray the Knowers to death. And you know the terrible tragedy of the Templars — they who had some knowledge of the hidden Mysteries — for under torture there were some who declared fragments of knowledge which were used to condemn. You remember how under torture it was declared more than once that when a Templar was initiated into the Mysteries he had to tread upon the Cross, and this was condemned as a sign of blasphemy, it was taken as a sign of unbelief. It was really the sign that the man relied upon the Cross to raise him up to knowledge, and if his feet for a moment were set upon it, it was in order that the Cross might rise with him upon it, and so carry him upon it, and so carry him upwards to a purer air, where some of the lower Mysteries were revealed. And one way of symbolism, and one great body which has come down from those days of the disappearance of the Mysteries, though most of its brethren know not what they possess — they know symbols only but seldom know the reality which these symbols express to the wise — is the great Brotherhood of Freemasonry, scattered over the world, who have kept in symbol what they have lost in knowledge, in order that they, in the days when knowledge returns, may bear testimony that it has never entirely passed away from earth. And those who belong to that Brotherhood will understand what I mean when I say that the treading on the Cross was no outrage, but the entrance over the threshold of knowledge.

And we find as we look backwards that there was a day when Christian Rosenkreuz came from the East to Europe and founded the first open Rosicrucian Society. I call it "open" because it is known to history, though foolish people think that it is myth and not history, forgetting that often myth and legend are the history of the great truth that lies behind. For he was a disciple of the Wisdom sent out by the Brotherhood to bring back the light of knowledge to Europe, and it was from that early Rosicrucian Society that the twelve brethren went out who brought back to Europe the bases of science, who brought alchemy and through that made chemistry possible, who taught astrology and so led on to astronomy, laying the bases of the modern knowledge. For real knowledge begins in the subtler and comes down to the denser world, and it does not begin in the denser and climb upwards to the subtler. And from that day began the re-dawn of science in Europe, and the possibility of knowledge gradually and slowly spreading. You can trace onwards Society after Society, all connected, though bearing different names, and ever teaching the same teachings — the preparation of Europe for the Restoration of the Mysteries in the wider and more effective fashion.

Then you come to the seventeenth and eighteenth centuries, where you have that mysterious Being the Comte de Germain, and where you find him working with our H. P. B., then a member of a great Austrian family still known by the name of Zimsky. You see those two brethren, disciples of the great Lodge, working along hand-in-hand that Europe might grow in knowledge. Then you come to a barrier that was set; for they were trying to change things by knowledge, and the knowledge came into the hands of those not yet fitted to receive it, and the starvation of the people and the misery of the nations, the tyranny and the suffering and the corruption both in Church and State, those were too strong for the teachers who where endeavoring in the world to guide men to knowledge, and the great outburst of the French Revolution poured forth a stream of blood which prevented further teaching along the inner lines. But still to some, here and there, it came, until the day dawned when those same teachers, brethren of the past, began again their work. That which failed in the eighteenth century was begun, in the nineteenth, and the bases of the Theosophical Society were laid and worked for by them, one hidden — for He had passed over the threshold into Masterhood and no longer worked openly among men — and the other, that noble Russian woman, H. P. Blavatsky, to whom the Theosophical Society owed its foundation and still largely owes its life. Then began the preparation for the Restoration of the Mysteries. And then that Brother whom a Master spoke of as "the Brother whom you know as H. P. B. but we otherwise" — he began again, by making a preparatory School within the Society, to lay the foundation of the Mysteries which later will be fully restored in our midst.

For then again, for the first time since from Europe they disappeared, the open way was shown whereon men might walk, and this Theosophical Society of ours, pointing to the Masters who founded it, pointing to the School made by Their messenger, shows the way along which the pupil may begin to walk, until he comes to the gateway of the true Mysteries; the way again is proclaimed and the Teachers are ready to teach.

Once more did the cry go out over the outer world, which you may read in Hindu Scripture: "Awake, arise, seek the great Teachers and attend; for the road, it is said, is narrow and sharp as the edge of a razor." That cry has gone out again, and there are ears to hear, ears that are able to hear the call, lips ready to answer. So in our days and our time, in the many nations of this mortal world, pupils are being found, pupils are being trained, in order that gradually it may be possible to restore the Mysteries as they were in the past, the gateways to the true Mysteries of the Brotherhood.

There you have the inner side of this great movement to which you all belong; and if you look upon the outer world you will see that, in many ways and along many lines, forces are being sent out to prepare the minds of the people at large for a higher and a more spiritual view of life, for a deeper and therefore truer view of human nature. For do not think that the influence of the Masters is limited within the limit of our Theosophical Society; that is Their messenger to the world, the vessel that They have chosen, into which They have poured Their Life; but far over the world Their Life also extends; for just as you may gather together in a reservoir water which shall then be taken from the reservoir and sent far and wide among the people who need it, so it is with this Life; as the rain comes down from the clouds over the whole earth, and not only into the reservoir made to receive a store of waters, so does the Masters' Life pour over the world at large, although concentrated here in the reservoir of the Theosophical Society.

It is our glory that we know how we are working; it is our privilege to be self-conscious co-operators in the working out of the Plan that the Masters are laboring to bring about successfully upon our earth. But we never dare to limit Them nor Their power, Their love nor Their compassion, and They can bring people whence They will, although an open way today is shown whereon surely They will be found.

And so, friends, I who have been bidden speak this word to all nations of the earth, speaking to you who are members of this Society that is Their servant in the lower world, I would say to you, that great are the possibilities that are being unveiled before you, great the avenues of progress which lie open before you today. It is true that you may come into the Society without any belief in the Masters of the Wisdom. It is true that you need not accept any doctrine, reincarnation, karma, or anything else, before you are admissible to the Society. That is true; but also it is true that there are those who know, those who are sent to do this work, those have a right to speak of what they know, and to repeat in the lower world what they have heard in the worlds beyond the physical.

And so it is that the road is open. The outer gate is wide and all who will may enter in. But to the Mysteries it is not so: straight is the gate and narrow is the way that leadeth unto Life Eternal and few there be that find it. Few at present, but to be more and more numerous as years go on; few today, but to increase to many in the days to come.

For there are great forces pouring down upon our world; the gates of the heavenly world are open, and life and power pour down upon the world of men. Well is it for you that your karma has brought you to birth in these happy days; well for you to be in them; but a thousand-fold the better, if within you the intuition which is the voice of the Spirit speaks, so that you may answer to the call of the Masters and find your way to Their feet.

THE VALUE OF DEVOTION

Among the many forces, which inspire men to activity, none, perhaps, plays a greater part than the feeling we call devotion — together with some feelings that often mask themselves under its name, though fundamentally differing from it in essence. The most heroic self-sacrifices have been inspired by it, while the most terrible sacrifices of others have been brought about by its pseudo-sister, fanaticism. It is as powerful a lever for raising a man as is the other for his degradation. The two sway mankind with overmastering power, and in some of their manifestations show an illusory resemblance; but the one has its roots in knowledge, the other in ignorance; the one bears the fruits of love, the other the poison-apples of hate.

A clear understanding of the nature of devotion is necessary, ere we are in a position to weigh its value and to distinguish it from the false Duessa. We must trace it to its origin in human nature, and see in what part of that nature it takes its rise. We must know in order that we may practice; for as knowledge without practice is barren, so practice without knowledge is wasted. Emotion unregulated by knowledge, like a river overflowing its banks, spreads in every direction as a devastating flood, while emotion guided by knowledge is like the same river running in appointed channels and fertilizing the land through which it flows.

If we study the inner nature of man, we find that it readily reveals three marked aspects that are distinguished from each other as the spiritual, the intellectual, and the emotional. On studying these further, we learn that the spiritual nature is that in which all the separate individualities inhere, that it is the common root, the unifying influence, that principle which, when developed, enables a man to realize in consciousness the oneness of all that lives. The intellectual nature may be said to be its antithesis; it is the individualizing force in man, that which makes the many from the One. Its self-realization is *I* and from this it sharply divides the *not-I*. It knows itself apart, separate, and works best in isolation, drawn inwards, self-concentrated, indifferent to all without. Not herein can be found the root of devotion, of a feeling, which rushes outward; intellect can grasp, it cannot move. Remains the emotional nature, the energizing force that causes action, that which feels. That it is which attracts us to an object, or repels us from it, and herein we shall find that devotion has its source. For as we study the emotional nature we see that it has two emotions — attraction and repulsion. It is ever moving us towards or away from objects surrounding us, according as those objects afford us pleasure or pain. All the feelings, which draw us towards another, fall under the head of attraction, and are forms of Love. All those, which repel us from another, fall under the head of repulsion, and are forms of Hate.

Now love takes different forms, and is called by different names, according as its object is above it, equal with it, or below it. Directed to those below it we name it pity, compassion, benevolence; directed to those equal with it, we call it friendship, passion, affection; directed to those above it, we style it reverence, adoration, devotion. Thus we trace devotion to its origin in the love-side of the emotional nature, and we define it as love directed to an object superior to the lover. When love is directed to the Teacher, to God, we rightly term it devotion; for then it is poured out before the superior, and shows in perfection the characteristic of all love given to those who are greater than ourselves, the characteristic of self- surrender.

Here we have the touchstone by which we can separate it from the fanaticism, which has inspired religious wars, religious persecutions religious animosities. These have their roots in hatred, not in love; they repel us from others instead of drawing us towards them. In the name of love to God, men injure their fellows; but when we analyze the motive power of their actions we do not find it in their love, but in their sense that they are right and others wrong, in the separateness they feel from others, in the feeling of repulsion from them because of their supposed wrongness, *i.e.,* in hate. Out of this come the bitter waters that sterilize the heart over which they flow. By this we can judge what we regard as devotion in ourselves; if it makes us humble, gentle, tolerant, friendly to all, then is it true devotion; if it makes us proud, harsh, separate, suspicious of all, then, however fair its seeming, it is dross, not gold.

Now devotion being a form of love, it can only flow out when an object presents itself which is attractive in its own nature, *i.e.,* happiness-giving. All men seek happiness, and that attracts them, draws them towards itself, which seems to them to make for happiness. Happiness is the feeling which accompanies the increase of life, and true and permanent bliss lies in union with the Self, the All-life, in conscious Self-identification with and expansion into the All; all efforts after happiness are efforts to unite with objects in order to absorb their life, thereby expanding the life that absorbs them. Happiness results from this union, because thereby the feeling of life is increased. Fundamentally the impulse to union comes from the Self, seeking to overpass the barriers which separate his selves on the lower planes, and the attraction between selves is the seeking by the Self in each of the Self in the other. " Lo! not for the sake of the husband is the husband dear, but for the sake of the Self the husband is dear. Lo! not for the sake of the wife is the wife dear, but for the sake of the Self the wife is dear." And so also with sons, wealth, Brahmanas, Kshattriyas, the worlds, the Gods, the Vedas, the elements, until: "Lo! not for the sake of the All is the All dear, but for the sake of the Self the All is dear". The Self seeks the Self, and this is the universal search for happiness, ever frustrated by the clash of form with form, the obstruction of the vehicles in which the separated selves abide.

In order to draw out devotion, then, an object which is attractive must be presented to man, and we find such objects presented most completely in the revelations of the Supreme Self made through human form in the *God-Men* who appear from time to time — the Avataras, or Divine Incarnations. Such beings are rendered supremely attractive by the beauty of character They manifest, by the rays of the Self which shine through the human veil, imperfectly concealing their divine loveliness. When He who is Beauty and Love and Bliss shows a little portion of Himself on earth, encased in human form, the weary eyes of men light up, the tired hearts of men expand, with a new hope, a new vigor. They are irresistibly attracted to Him; devotion spontaneously springs up. Among Christians the intensity of religious devotion flows out to Christ, the Divine Man regarded as an incarnation of Deity, far more than to *God* in the abstract. It is His human side, His life and death, His sympathy and compassion, His gentle wisdom and patient sufferings, which stir men's hearts to a passion of devotion; as the *Man of Sorrows* the innocent and willing Sufferer, He wins perennially the love of men; it is the memory of Him as Man that holds men captive; as phrased by one of His devotees:

> *The Cross of Christ*
> *Is more to us than all His miracles.*

And so in the God-Men of other faiths; it is Shri Rama the Divine King, Shri Krshna the Friend and Lover, who win the undying, passionate devotion of millions of human hearts. They render Deity attractive by softening its dazzling radiance into a light that human eyes can bear as it shines through the veil of humanity; they limit the divine attributes till they become small enough for the human intelligence to grasp. These stand as Objects of devotion, attracting love by Their perfect loveableness; They need only to be seen to be loved; where They are not loved it is merely because They are not seen. Devotion to Divine Men is not a matter for discussion or for argument; the moment one of Them is seen by the inner vision, the heart rushes out to Him and falls unbidden at His feet. Devotion may be cultivated by the reason, may be approved of and nurtured by the intelligence; but its primary impulse comes from the heart, not from the head, and flows out spontaneously to the Object that attracts it, to the shining of the Self through a translucent veil, to the Heart's Desire in manifested form.

Next, as objects of devotion, come the Teachers who, having Themselves obtained liberation, remain voluntarily within touch of humanity, retaining human bodies while the Jivatma enjoys nirvanic consciousness. They stand, as it were, between the Avataras and the earthly teachers who are Their disciples, and who have not yet reached liberation; but to the eyes of men on earth They are scarce distinguishable from the Avataras Themselves, and They draw men with the same overmastering attraction. The Avatara truly is greater, but that greatness lies on the side turned away from earth, and we can imagine no completer perfection than that of the Masters of the Wisdom.

Then come, in more constant physical communication with men, the teachers who are the immediate spiritual guides of those whose faces are turned to the steep path that leads to the heights, to the snowy mountains of human perfection. Still marred by weaknesses though they be, these have advanced sufficiently beyond their fellow-men to serve as their guides and helpers; and for the most part the earlier stages of progress are trodden by devotion to them. Further, as they are near the threshold of liberation, they will shortly pass into the class beyond them, and, as spiritual links are imperishable, will then be able, with added force, to draw their devotees after them. Love given to them strengthens and expands the nature of their lovers, and there is no surer path to devotion, in its highest meaning, than the love and trust given to the earthly teacher. Nowhere has this been realized so strongly as in the East, where the love and service of the teacher have ever been held as necessary to spiritual progress. Much of the decay of modern India is due to the ignorance, the pride, the unspirituality of those who still wear the ancient name while devoid of all the qualities once implied by it; for as the best wine makes the sharpest vinegar, so is the degradation of the highest the lowest depth.

How shall devotion, then, be evoked and nourished? Only by meeting in the outer or inner world a fit object of devotion, and by yielding fully and unreservedly to the attraction it exercises. The glad and cordial recognition of excellence wherever found, the checking of the critical and carping spirit that fixes on defects and ignores virtues, these things prepare the soul to recognize his teacher when he appears. Many a one misses his teacher by the mental habit of fixing the attention on blemishes rather than on beauties, by seeing only the sun-spots and not the Sun. Further, the recognition of excellence shows the capacity to reproduce it; sympathetic vibrations are given out only by a string tuned to produce by itself a similar note; the soul knows his kin, even though they be older than himself, and only those akin to greatness are wakened by the great to response.

When the teacher is found and the tie with him is made, the first great step is taken. Then follows the steady culture of devotion to him, and through him to Those beyond and to the Supreme Self, manifested in form. This must never be forgotten, for the teacher is a means not an end, a transmitter not an originator of the divine light, a moon not a sun. He helps, strengthens, guides, evolves his pupil; but the end is the shining out of the Self in the disciple, the Self who is one, and is in teacher and disciple alike.

Devotion to the embodiment of the Self spoken of as the Avatara may be nourished and increased by reading and meditating on His sayings and the incidents of His life on earth. It is a good plan to read over an incident and then vividly picture it in the mind, using the imagination to produce a full and detailed picture, and feeling one's self as present in it, a spectator or an actor therein. This "scientific use of the imagination" is a great provocative of devotion, and it actually brings the devotee into touch with the scene depicted; so that he may one day find himself scanning the akashic record of the event, a very part of that living picture, learning undreamed-of lessons from his presence there.

Another way of cultivating devotion is to be much in company with those in whom devotion burns more brightly than in ourselves. As burning wood thrown into a smoldering fire will cause a flame to burst out brightly again, so the nearness of the warm fire of devotion in another rekindles the flagging energy of a weaker soul. Here again the disciple may gain much by frequenting the company of his teacher whose steadier force will energize his own.

Narada, in his admirable Sutras, thus instructs us on the culture of devotion, and who should teach better than that ideal devotee?

Almost needless to add that the direct contemplation of, meditation on, and adoration of, the object of devotion quicken and intensify the love. In the hurry of modern life we are apt to forget the power of quiet thought, and to grudge the time necessary for its exercise. Thought of the one we love increases love, and the would-be devotee must give time to the object of his devotion; and it is not his thought alone that is at work. As little can a plant grow without sunlight, as devotion without the warming and energizing rays that stream from its object; the older soul pours out far more love than he receives, and his light and heat permeate and strengthen the younger soul. The teacher loves his disciple, and God loves His devotee, far more than the disciple loves his teacher, or the devotee his God. The love of the devotee for his Lord is but a faint reflection of the love of Him who is Love itself. It is said that if a child throws a pebble to the ground, the whole great earth moves towards the pebble as well as draws the pebble to itself; attraction cannot be one-sided. In the spiritual world when man makes one step towards God, God makes a hundred steps towards man, for greatness there means greatness in giving, and the ocean pours forth its measureless depths towards any drop that seeks its bosom.

Having seen what devotion is, what its objects are, how it can be increased, we may fitly measure its value so as to find motive for attaining it.

Devotion changes the devotee into the likeness of the one he loves. Solomon, the wise Hebrew, declares that "as a man thinks so he is". The *Chhandogyopanishad* teaches that "man is created by thought; what he thinks of, that he becomes". But the intellect alone cannot easily be shaped into the likeness of the Supreme. As cold iron is hard, and incapable of being worked, but heated in the furnace becomes fluid and flows readily into any desired mold, so is it with the intellect. It must be melted in the fire of devotion, and then it will quickly be shaped into the likeness of the Beloved. Even love between equals, where it is strong and faithful and long-continued, molds them into each other's likeness; husband and wife become like each other, close friends grow similar each to each. And love directed to one above us exercises its transforming power still more forcibly, and easily shapes the nature it renders plastic into the likeness, which is enshrined in the heart.

Devotion prevents the making of new karma, and when the old is exhausted the devotee is free. The great Christian teacher, S. Paul, writing of himself, declared that he no longer lived but Christ lived in him; and this saying becomes true of each devotee as his devotion leads him to surrender himself utterly to the one he loves. He thinks of his body not as his, but as an instrument used by his Lord for the world's helping; all his actions are done because they are the duty given him by his Beloved; does he eat, it is not to gratify the palate, but to keep in working order his Lord's instrument; does he think, it is not for the pleasure of thinking, but in order that his Lord's work may be the better done; he merges his life in the life he loves, thinks, works, acts, in union with that higher life, merging his smaller rill of being in the larger stream, and finding a deep joy in feeling himself part of the fuller life. So it is written: " Whatsoever thou doest, whatsoever thou eatest, whatsoever thou offerest, whatsoever thou givest, whatsoever them doest of austerity, 0 son of Kunti, do thou that as an offering unto Me. Thus shalt thou be liberated from the bonds of action (yielding) good and evil fruits" (Bhagavad-Gita, ix. 27, 28). Where fruits of action are not desired, where actions are done only as sacrifice, no karma is made by the actor, and he is not bound by them to the wheel of births and deaths.

Devotion cleanses the heart. Once again Shri Krshna teaches us, and the words at first seem strange: "Even if the most sinful worship me with undivided heart, he too must be accounted righteous." Why? — we naturally ask; and the answer comes: " Because he hath rightly resolved *speedily he becometh dutiful,* and goeth to peace eternal" (Ibid. 30, 31). In the higher world men are judged by motives not by actions, by inner attitude not by external signs. When a man feels devotion to the Supreme, he has turned his back on evil and has turned his face to the goal; he may stumble, stray, even fall, but his face is turned in the right direction, he is going homewards; he must needs become dutiful by the force of his devotion, for seeking union with his Beloved he will swiftly cast away everything that prevents the union; to Him who sees the end from the beginning he *is* righteous when his face is turned to righteousness; his love will burn up in him the evil that veils from him the Being he adores, and produce in him the likeness that he worships. So sure is this action, so inviolable the law, that he is *accounted righteous*. Of the two great classes of the self-seekers and the seekers of the Self, he has changed from the first into the second.

Devotion puts an end to pain. That which we do for the object of our love is done with joy, and pain is merged in gladness when it is endured for the sake of the one we love. The mere earthly lover will gladly undergo hardships, perils, sufferings, to win approval from, or to gain something desirable for, his beloved. Why should not the one who has caught a glimpse of the beauty of the Self do joyfully all that brings him nearer to union, sacrifice ungrudgingly, nay, with delight, all that withholds him from the bridal of the inner life? For the sake of being with one we love, we readily endure inconvenience, sacrifice comfort, the joy of the presence of the loved one lending charm to the surmounting of all obstacles that separate. Thus devotion makes hard things easy, and painful things pleasant. For love is the world- alchemist and transmutes all to gold.

Devotion gives peace. The heart at peace in the Self is at peace with all. The devotee sees the Self in all; all forms around him bear the impress of the Beloved. How then can he hate or despise or repel any, when the Face he loves smiles at him behind every mask? "Sages look with equal eye on a Brahmana adorned with learning and humility, on a cow, an elephant, and even a dog and a dog-eater" (Bhagavad-Gita, v. 18). No one, nothing, can be outside the heart of the devotee, since nothing is outside the embrace of his Lord. If we love the very objects touched by the one we love, how shall we not love all forms in which the Beloved is enshrined? A child in his play may draw over his laughing face a hideous mask, but the mother knows her darling is underneath; and when in the world-lila the Lord is hidden under forms repulsive, His lovers are not repelled, but see only Him. There is no creature, moving or unmoving, that exists bereft of Him, and in the heart-chamber of the vilest sinner the Holiest abides.

Thus we return, to our starting-point and learn to recognize the devotee by his aspect to his fellow- creatures. His abounding love, his tenderness, his compassion, his pity, his sympathy with all faiths and all ideals, these mark him out as a lover of the Lord of Love. It is told of Shri Ramanujacharya that a mantra was once given him by his Guru, and he asked what would happen if he told it to another: "Thou wilt die," was the answer. "And what will happen to the one who hears it?" "He will be liberated." Then out ran the devotee of Shri Krshna, and, flying to the top of a tower, he shouted out the mantra to the crowded streets below, careless what happened to himself so that others should be set free from sin and sorrow. There is the typical devotee, there the lover transformed into the likeness of the Beloved.

www.ingramcontent.com/pod-product-compliance
Lightning Source LLC
LaVergne TN
LVHW041502070426
835507LV00009B/772